CHINESE
HOROSCOPES
FOR
LOVERS

The
Monkey

LORI REID

illustrated by
PAUL COLLICUTT

ELEMENT BOOKS

Shaftesbury, Dorset • Rockport, Massachusetts • Brisbane, Queensland

First published in Great Britain in 1996 by

ELEMENT BOOKS LIMITED

Shaftesbury, Dorset SP7 8BP

Published in the USA in 1996 by

ELEMENT BOOKS, INC.

PO Box 830, Rockport, MA 01966

Published in Australia in 1996 by

ELEMENT BOOKS LIMITED

for JACARANDA WILEY LIMITED

33 Park Road, Milton, Brisbane 4064

Designed and created by

THE BRIDGEWATER BOOK COMPANY

Art directed by *Peter Bridgewater*

Designed by *Angela Neal*

Picture research by *Vanessa Fletcher*

Edited by *Gillian Delaforce*

Printed and bound in Great Britain by
BPC Paulton Books Ltd

British Library Cataloguing in Publication data available

Library of Congress Cataloging in Publication data available

ISBN 1-85230-769-2

Contents

THE
MONKEY

猴

8

*Why are
some people
lucky in
love and
others not?*

Chinese Astrology

SOME PEOPLE fall in love and, as the fairy tales go, live happily ever after. Others fall in love – again and again, make the same mistakes every time and never form a lasting relationship. Most of us come between these two extremes,

and some people form remarkably successful unions while others make spectacular disasters of their personal lives. Why are some people lucky in love while others have the odds stacked against them?

ANIMAL NAMES

According to the philosophy of the Far East, luck has very little to do with it. The answer, the philosophers say, lies with 'the Animal that hides in our hearts'. This Animal, of which there are 12, forms part of the complex art of Chinese Astrology. Each year of a 12-year cycle is attributed an Animal sign, whose characteristics are said to influence worldly events as well as the personality and fate of each living thing that comes under its dominion. The 12 Animals run in sequence, beginning with the Rat and followed by the Ox, Tiger, Rabbit, Dragon, Snake, Horse, Sheep, Monkey, Rooster, Dog and last, but not least, the Pig. Being born in the Year of the Ox, for example, is simply a way of describing what you're like, physically and psychologically. And this is quite different from someone who, for instance, is born in the Year of the Snake.

猴

9

*The 12
Animals
of Chinese
Astrology.*

RELATIONSHIPS

These Animal names are merely the tip of the ice-
berg, considering the complexity of the whole
subject. Yet such are the richness and wisdom of Chinese
Astrology that understanding the principles behind the year in
which you were born will give you powerful insights into your
own personality. The system is very specific about which Animals
are compatible and which are antagonistic and this tells us
whether our relationships will be successful. Marriages are made
in heaven, so the saying goes. The heavens, according to Chinese
beliefs, can point the way. The rest is up to us.

Year Chart and Birth Dates

UNLIKE THE WESTERN CALENDAR, which is based on the Sun, the Oriental year is based on the movement of the Moon, which means that New Year's Day does not fall on a fixed date. This Year Chart, taken from the Chinese Perpetual Calendar, lists the dates on which each year begins and ends together with its Animal ruler for the year. In addition, the Chinese believe that the tangible world is composed of 5 elements, each slightly adapting the characteristics of the Animal signs. These elemental influences are also given here. Finally, the aspect, that is, whether the year is characteristically Yin (-) or Yang (+), is also listed.

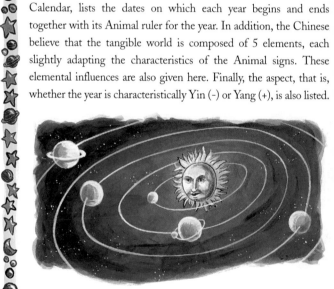

The Western calendar is based on the Sun; the Oriental on the Moon.

YIN AND YANG

Yin and Yang are the terms given to the dynamic complementary forces that keep the universe in balance and which are the central principles behind life. Yin is all that is considered negative, passive, feminine, night, the Moon, while Yang is considered positive, active, masculine, day, the Sun.

猴

11

Year	From – To	Animal sign	Element	Aspect
1900	31 Jan 1900 – 18 Feb 1901	Rat	Metal	+ Yang
1901	19 Feb 1901 – 7 Feb 1902	Ox	Metal	– Yin
1902	8 Feb 1902 – 28 Jan 1903	Tiger	Water	+ Yang
1903	29 Jan 1903 – 15 Feb 1904	Rabbit	Water	– Yin
1904	16 Feb 1904 – 3 Feb 1905	Dragon	Wood	+ Yang
1905	4 Feb 1905 – 24 Jan 1906	Snake	Wood	– Yin
1906	25 Jan 1906 – 12 Feb 1907	Horse	Fire	+ Yang
1907	13 Feb 1907 – 1 Feb 1908	Sheep	Fire	– Yin
1908	2 Feb 1908 – 21 Jan 1909	Monkey	Earth	+ Yang
1909	22 Jan 1909 – 9 Feb 1910	Rooster	Earth	– Yin
1910	10 Feb 1910 – 29 Jan 1911	Dog	Metal	+ Yang
1911	30 Jan 1911 – 17 Feb 1912	Pig	Metal	– Yin
1912	18 Feb 1912 – 5 Feb 1913	Rat	Water	+ Yang
1913	6 Feb 1913 – 25 Jan 1914	Ox	Water	– Yin
1914	26 Jan 1914 – 13 Feb 1915	Tiger	Wood	+ Yang
1915	14 Feb 1915 – 2 Feb 1916	Rabbit	Wood	– Yin
1916	3 Feb 1916 – 22 Jan 1917	Dragon	Fire	+ Yang
1917	23 Jan 1917 – 10 Feb 1918	Snake	Fire	– Yin
1918	11 Feb 1918 – 31 Jan 1919	Horse	Earth	+ Yang
1919	1 Feb 1919 – 19 Feb 1920	Sheep	Earth	– Yin
1920	20 Feb 1920 – 7 Feb 1921	Monkey	Metal	+ Yang
1921	8 Feb 1921 – 27 Jan 1922	Rooster	Metal	– Yin
1922	28 Jan 1922 – 15 Feb 1923	Dog	Water	+ Yang
1923	16 Feb 1923 – 4 Feb 1924	Pig	Water	– Yin
1924	5 Feb 1924 – 24 Jan 1925	Rat	Wood	+ Yang
1925	25 Jan 1925 – 12 Feb 1926	Ox	Wood	– Yin
1926	13 Feb 1926 – 1 Feb 1927	Tiger	Fire	+ Yang
1927	2 Feb 1927 – 22 Jan 1928	Rabbit	Fire	– Yin
1928	23 Jan 1928 – 9 Feb 1929	Dragon	Earth	+ Yang
1929	10 Feb 1929 – 29 Jan 1930	Snake	Earth	– Yin
1930	30 Jan 1930 – 16 Feb 1931	Horse	Metal	+ Yang
1931	17 Feb 1931 – 5 Feb 1932	Sheep	Metal	– Yin
1932	6 Feb 1932 – 25 Jan 1933	Monkey	Water	+ Yang
1933	26 Jan 1933 – 13 Feb 1934	Rooster	Water	– Yin
1934	14 Feb 1934 – 3 Feb 1935	Dog	Wood	+ Yang
1935	4 Feb 1935 – 23 Jan 1936	Pig	Wood	– Yin

猴

12

Year	From – To	Animal sign	Element	Aspect
1936	24 Jan 1936 – 10 Feb 1937	Rat	Fire	+ Yang
1937	11 Feb 1937 – 30 Jan 1938	Ox	Fire	− Yin
1938	31 Jan 1938 – 18 Feb 1939	Tiger	Earth	+ Yang
1939	19 Feb 1939 – 7 Feb 1940	Rabbit	Earth	− Yin
1940	8 Feb 1940 – 26 Jan 1941	Dragon	Metal	+ Yang
1941	27 Jan 1941 – 14 Feb 1942	Snake	Metal	− Yin
1942	15 Feb 1942 – 4 Feb 1943	Horse	Water	+ Yang
1943	5 Feb 1943 – 24 Jan 1944	Sheep	Water	− Yin
1944	25 Jan 1944 – 12 Feb 1945	Monkey	Wood	+ Yang
1945	13 Feb 1945 – 1 Feb 1946	Rooster	Wood	− Yin
1946	2 Feb 1946 – 21 Jan 1947	Dog	Fire	+ Yang
1947	22 Jan 1947 – 9 Feb 1948	Pig	Fire	− Yin
1948	10 Feb 1948 – 28 Jan 1949	Rat	Earth	+ Yang
1949	29 Jan 1949 – 16 Feb 1950	Ox	Earth	− Yin
1950	17 Feb 1950 – 5 Feb 1951	Tiger	Metal	+ Yang
1951	6 Feb 1951 – 26 Jan 1952	Rabbit	Metal	− Yin
1952	27 Jan 1952 – 13 Feb 1953	Dragon	Water	+ Yang
1953	14 Feb 1953 – 2 Feb 1954	Snake	Water	− Yin
1954	3 Feb 1954 – 23 Jan 1955	Horse	Wood	+ Yang
1955	24 Jan 1955 – 11 Feb 1956	Sheep	Wood	− Yin
1956	12 Feb 1956 – 30 Jan 1957	Monkey	Fire	+ Yang
1957	31 Jan 1957 – 17 Feb 1958	Rooster	Fire	− Yin
1958	18 Feb 1958 – 7 Feb 1959	Dog	Earth	+ Yang
1959	8 Feb 1959 – 27 Jan 1960	Pig	Earth	− Yin
1960	28 Jan 1960 – 14 Feb 1961	Rat	Metal	+ Yang
1961	15 Feb 1961 – 4 Feb 1962	Ox	Metal	− Yin
1962	5 Feb 1962 – 24 Jan 1963	Tiger	Water	+ Yang
1963	25 Jan 1963 – 12 Feb 1964	Rabbit	Water	− Yin
1964	13 Feb 1964 – 1 Feb 1965	Dragon	Wood	+ Yang
1965	2 Feb 1965 – 20 Jan 1966	Snake	Wood	− Yin
1966	21 Jan 1966 – 8 Feb 1967	Horse	Fire	+ Yang
1967	9 Feb 1967 – 29 Jan 1968	Sheep	Fire	− Yin
1968	30 Jan 1968 – 16 Feb 1969	Monkey	Earth	+ Yang
1969	17 Feb 1969 – 5 Feb 1970	Rooster	Earth	− Yin
1970	6 Feb 1970 – 26 Jan 1971	Dog	Metal	+ Yang
1971	27 Jan 1971 – 15 Jan 1972	Pig	Metal	− Yin

Year	From – To		Animal sign	Element	Aspect	
1972	16 Jan 1972 – 2 Feb 1973		Rat	Water	+	Yang
1973	3 Feb 1973 – 22 Jan 1974		Ox	Water	–	Yin
1974	23 Jan 1974 – 10 Feb 1975		Tiger	Wood	+	Yang
1975	11 Feb 1975 – 30 Jan 1976		Rabbit	Wood	–	Yin
1976	31 Jan 1976 – 17 Feb 1977		Dragon	Fire	+	Yang
1977	18 Feb 1977 – 6 Feb 1978		Snake	Fire	–	Yin
1978	7 Feb 1978 – 27 Jan 1979		Horse	Earth	+	Yang
1979	28 Jan 1979 – 15 Feb 1980		Sheep	Earth	–	Yin
1980	16 Feb 1980 – 4 Feb 1981		Monkey	Metal	+	Yang
1981	5 Feb 1981 – 24 Jan 1982		Rooster	Metal	–	Yin
1982	25 Jan 1982 – 12 Feb 1983		Dog	Water	+	Yang
1983	13 Feb 1983 – 1 Feb 1984		Pig	Water	–	Yin
1984	2 Feb 1984 – 19 Feb 1985		Rat	Wood	+	Yang
1985	20 Feb 1985 – 8 Feb 1986		Ox	Wood	–	Yin
1986	9 Feb 1986 – 28 Jan 1987		Tiger	Fire	+	Yang
1987	29 Jan 1987 – 16 Feb 1988		Rabbit	Fire	–	Yin
1988	17 Feb 1988 – 5 Feb 1989		Dragon	Earth	+	Yang
1989	6 Feb 1989 – 26 Jan 1990		Snake	Earth	–	Yin
1990	27 Jan 1990 – 14 Feb 1991		Horse	Metal	+	Yang
1991	15 Feb 1991 – 3 Feb 1992		Sheep	Metal	–	Yin
1992	4 Feb 1992 – 22 Jan 1993		Monkey	Water	+	Yang
1993	23 Jan 1993 – 9 Feb 1994		Rooster	Water	–	Yin
1994	10 Feb 1994 – 30 Jan 1995		Dog	Wood	+	Yang
1995	31 Jan 1995 – 18 Feb 1996		Pig	Wood	–	Yin
1996	19 Feb 1996 – 7 Feb 1997		Rat	Fire	+	Yang
1997	8 Feb 1997 – 27 Jan 1998		Ox	Fire	–	Yin
1998	28 Jan 1998 – 15 Feb 1999		Tiger	Earth	+	Yang
1999	16 Feb 1999 – 4 Feb 2000		Rabbit	Earth	–	Yin
2000	5 Feb 2000 – 23 Jan 2001		Dragon	Metal	+	Yang
2001	24 Jan 2001 – 11 Feb 2002		Snake	Metal	–	Yin
2002	12 Feb 2002 – 31 Jan 2003		Horse	Water	+	Yang
2003	1 Feb 2003 – 21 Jan 2004		Sheep	Water	–	Yin
2004	22 Jan 2004 – 8 Feb 2005		Monkey	Wood	+	Yang
2005	9 Feb 2005 – 28 Jan 2006		Rooster	Wood	–	Yin
2006	29 Jan 2006 – 17 Feb 2007		Dog	Fire	+	Yang
2007	18 Feb 2007 – 6 Feb 2008		Pig	Fire	–	Yin

13

14

Introducing the Animals

| THE RAT | ♥ ♥ ♥ DRAGON, MONKEY | ✖ HORSE |

Outwardly cool, Rats are passionate lovers with depths of feeling that others don't often recognize. Rats are very self-controlled.

| THE OX | ♥ ♥ ♥ SNAKE, ROOSTER | ✖ SHEEP |

Not necessarily the most romantic of the signs, Ox people make steadfast lovers as well as faithful, affectionate partners.

| THE TIGER | ♥ ♥ ♥ HORSE, DOG | ✖ MONKEY |

Passionate and sensual, Tigers are exciting lovers. Flirty when young, once committed they make stable partners and keep their sexual allure.

| THE RABBIT | ♥ ♥ ♥ SHEEP, PIG | ✖ ROOSTER |

Gentle, emotional and sentimental, Rabbits make sensitive lovers. They are shrewd and seek a partner who offers security.

| THE DRAGON | ♥ ♥ ♥ RAT, MONKEY | ✖ DOG |

Dragon folk get as much stimulation from mind-touch as they do through sex. A partner on the same wave-length is essential.

| THE SNAKE | ♥ ♥ ♥ OX, ROOSTER | ✖ PIG |

Deeply passionate, strongly sexed but not aggressive, snakes are attracted to elegant, refined partners. But they are deeply jealous and possessive.

♥ ♥ ♥ COMPATIBLE   ✖ INCOMPATIBLE

15

| THE HORSE | ♥ ♥ ♥ TIGER, DOG | ✖ RAT |

For horse-born folk love is blind. In losing their hearts, they lose their heads and make several mistakes before finding the right partner.

| THE SHEEP | ♥ ♥ ♥ RABBIT, PIG | ✖ OX |

Sheep-born people are made for marriage. Domesticated home-lovers, they find emotional satisfaction with a partner who provides security.

| THE MONKEY | ♥ ♥ ♥ DRAGON, RAT | ✖ TIGER |

Clever and witty, Monkeys need partners who will keep them stimulated. Forget the 9 to 5 routine, these people need *pizzazz*.

| THE ROOSTER | ♥ ♥ ♥ OX, SNAKE | ✖ RABBIT |

The Rooster's stylish good looks guarantee they will attract many suitors. They are level-headed and approach relationships coolly.

| THE DOG | ♥ ♥ ♥ TIGER, HORSE | ✖ DRAGON |

A loving, stable relationship is an essential component in the lives of Dogs. Once they have found their mate, they remain faithful for life.

| THE PIG | ♥ ♥ ♥ RABBIT, SHEEP | ✖ SNAKE |

These are sensual hedonists who enjoy lingering love-making between satin sheets. Caviar and champagne go down very nicely too.

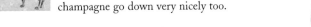

The Monkey Personality

猴

16

YEARS OF THE MONKEY

1908 ★ 1920 ★ 1932 ★ 1944 ★ 1956 ★ 1968
1980 ★ 1992 ★ 2004

QUICK WITS and mental dexterity are the Monkey trademarks, and you pride yourself that you can dance rings around everyone else. And you can. With your clever, alert mind, you catch on at a glance and process information in a trice. You're bright as a button, nimble of foot, and can turn your hand to almost any task; the more intricate and involved the better. With your razor-sharp mind, you're constantly seeking new experiences and fresh challenges to stimulate your senses.

MONKEY FACTS

Ninth in order ★ *Chinese name – HOU* ★ *Sign of imagination*
★ *Hour – 3PM– 4.59PM* ★ *Month – August* ★
★ *Western counterpart – Leo* ★

CHARACTERISTICS

♥ *Imagination* ♥ *Ingenuity* ♥ *Resourcefulness* ♥ *Versatility*
♥ *Persuasiveness* ♥ *Sense of humour*

✖ *Mischievousness* ✖ *Slyness* ✖ *Restlessness* ✖ *Impudence*
✖ *Superficiality* ✖ *Mendacity*

Clever dextrous Monkeys can turn their nimble fingers to any task.

THE JOKER

You possess an irrepressible sense of fun, delighting in jokes, tricks and amusing stories. But you can also be a bit of a rascal – especially when you're bored. That's when you get that mischievous glint in your eye and simply have to go and stir something or *someone* up just for the sheer hell of it! Then you take a front-row seat and settle down to enjoy the fireworks.

Naughty Monkeys love to throw custard pies in the face of convention.

MONKEY CURIOSITY

Some people call it inquisitiveness. Others swear it's downright nosiness. *You* say that you're simply displaying a healthy interest. However you want to label it, as a Monkey you have an insatiable curiosity about what's going on around you.

Your Hour of Birth

WHILE YOUR YEAR OF BIRTH describes your fundamental character, the Animal governing the actual hour in which you were born describes your outer temperament, how people see you or the picture you present to the outside world. Note that each Animal rules over two consecutive hours. Also note that these are GMT standard times and that adjustments need to be made if you were born during Summer or daylight saving time.

11PM – 12.59AM ★ RAT

Pleasant, sociable, easy to get on with. An active, confident, busy person – and a bit of a busybody to boot.

1AM – 2.59AM ★ OX

Level-headed and down-to-earth, you come across as knowledgeable and reliable – sometimes, though, a bit biased.

3AM – 4.59AM ★ TIGER

Enthusiastic and self-assured, people see you as a strong and positive personality – at times a little over-exuberant.

5AM – 6.59AM ★ RABBIT

You're sensitive and shy and don't project your real self to the world. You feel you have to put on an act to please others.

7AM – 8.59AM ★ DRAGON

Independent and interesting, you present a picture of someone who is quite out of the ordinary.

9AM – 10.59AM ★ SNAKE

You can be a bit difficult to fathom and, because you appear so controlled, people either take to you instantly, or not at all.

 11AM – 12.59PM ★ HORSE
Open, cheerful and happy-go-lucky is the picture you always put across to others. You're an extrovert and it generally shows.

 5PM – 6.59PM ★ ROOSTER
There's something rather stylish in your approach that gives people an impression of elegance and glamour. But you don't suffer fools gladly.

 1PM – 2.59PM ★ SHEEP
Your unassuming nature won't allow you to foist yourself upon others so people see you as quiet and retiring – but eminently sensible, though.

 7PM – 8.59PM ★ DOG
Some people see you as steady and reliable, others as quiet and graceful and others still as dull and unimaginative. It all depends who you're with at the time.

 3PM – 4.59PM ★ MONKEY
Lively and talkative, that twinkle in your eye will guarantee you make friends wherever you go.

 9PM – 10.59PM ★ PIG
Your laid-back manner conceals a depth of interest and intelligence that doesn't always come through at first glance.

YOUR HOUR OF BIRTH

19

Your hour of birth describes your outer temperament.

20

The Monkey Lover

All Monkeys are youthful and maintain their looks and sexual appetite well into their later years. But, more than that, because you're versatile and fun-loving you enjoy playing out all sorts of fantasy roles as part of your love-making. It's this that, in a long-term relationship, keeps your partner guessing and his or her interest from flagging; it keeps your partnership fresh and evergreen.

JUST AS you're fleet of foot and nimble of mind, so you can be fast and loose when it comes to sexual relationships. Indeed, of all the Astrological Animal signs, yours is the one that has the greatest reputation for promiscuity. Certainly you can be flirtatious, although in truth that applies more to your younger days. Perhaps it's something to do with boredom, or the need for new experiences. Or perhaps you see it as a skill, like a balancing act, to have several lovers and admirers on the go at the same time.

Weighing up prospective lovers is a favourite Monkey pastime.

MONKEY BUSINESS

The negative side of the Monkey character is your sense of mischief, delight in breaking the rules, cheeky impishness and ability to bend the truth to your own advantage. There are times when Monkey folk can be unscrupulous, manipulative and clever at covering up the traces – skills which they wouldn't baulk at using in the pursuit of a lover!

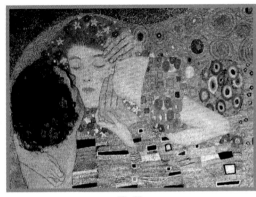

The Kiss
GUSTAV KLIMT 1862–1918

THE VAMP

As a lover you can be passionate and intense. You know how to be a vamp and a tease, how to give just the right cues as a come-on to your partner. You know how to charm and allure, how to be funny and provocative, how to amuse and entertain with your sparkling wit and ready repartee. Deeply sensual and fantastically sexy, you're hot stuff between the sheets. But when you settle down you're likely to remain remarkably faithful and true.

Monkeys in full flirt mode are irresistible.

22

In Your Element

ALTHOUGH YOUR SIGN recurs every 12 years, each generation is slightly modified by one of 5 elements. If you were born under the Metal influence your character, emotions and behaviour would show significant variations from an individual born under one of the other elements. Check the Year Chart for your ruling element and discover what effects it has upon you.

THE METAL MONKEY ★ 1920 AND 1980

Clever, persuasive and highly ambitious, in business you're a success story because you're prepared to put in a good deal of hard work in order to make it to the top. In love you're passionate, loyal and faithful.

THE WATER MONKEY ★ 1932 AND 1992

Water adds a strong sensitivity to your nature which means you can get easily hurt so you hide your feelings from others. If you concentrate and channel your intellectual energies you can become an original trend-setter and an inspiration to all. If not, you'll be fickle and indecisive.

23

THE WOOD MONKEY ★ 1944 AND 2004

With your logical mind it's in the world of communications, linguistics, computers and information technology that you excel. You have more integrity than most other Monkeys and a natural gift for dealing with people.

THE FIRE MONKEY ★ 1956

What stamina, what daring and what a uniquely inventive mind you possess! As a Fire Monkey you have a huge sex drive and love playing cat-and-mouse games with the opposite sex, but in the bedroom and the boardroom you will always strive to gain the upper hand.

THE EARTH MONKEY ★ 1908 AND 1968

Honest, serious, intelligent and academically-minded, you like to go by the rule-book. Emotionally reserved and controlled, you're less highly strung than most and altogether more dependable. As a partner you're kind and loyal, very loving and deeply understanding.

24

Rencontre
du Soir
(detail)
THEOPHILE-
ALEXANDRE
STEINLEN
1859–1923

Partners in Love

THE CHINESE are very definite about which animals are compatible with each other and which are antagonistic. So find out if you're truly suited to your partner.

MONKEY + RAT
★ *A shared outlook and a common understanding equals love for you and your Rat.*

MONKEY + OX
★ *When this relationship works, life can be fun, fun, fun.*

MONKEY + TIGER
★ *You're likely to drive each other up the wall!*

MONKEY + RABBIT
★ *It'll end in tears.*

MONKEY + DRAGON
★ *You think alike and understand each other perfectly – a combination destined to be happy and successful.*

MONKEY + SNAKE
★ *Intellectually, you make a great match. Emotionally, jealousy gets in the way.*

MONKEY + HORSE
★ *A prickly combination, better for friendship than for marriage.*

MONKEY + SHEEP
★ *Very different people, but you could make a go of it by pooling your talents and resources.*

The Monkey and the Sheep make a mutually supportive partnership.

LOVE PARTNERS AT A GLANCE

Monkey with:	Tips on Togetherness	Compatibility
Rat	irresistible magnetism	♥♥♥♥
Ox	a complementary match	♥♥
Tiger	deeply frustrating	♥
Rabbit	heartbreak hotel	♥
Dragon	refreshingly alive	♥♥♥♥
Snake	only with co-operation	♥♥
Horse	social yes, sexual no	♥♥
Sheep	learn from each other	♥♥
Monkey	together it's just one long summer holiday	♥♥♥♥
Rooster	soooo picky	♥
Dog	cheerfully complementary	♥♥♥
Pig	a colourful affair	♥♥♥

COMPATIBILITY RATINGS:
♥ *conflict*　♥♥ *work at it*　♥♥♥ *strong sexual attraction*　♥♥♥♥ *heavenly!*

MONKEY + MONKEY
★ *Brilliant rapport even if at times you behave like adolescents!*

Eiaha chipa
PAUL GAUGUIN 1848–1903

MONKEY + ROOSTER
★ *Romantically, this could be a bit of a damp squib.*

MONKEY + DOG
★ *Not a bad shot this. With so much desire to pull together, you've got plenty going for you.*

MONKEY + PIG
★ *Occasional strife heightens the sexual tension between you.*

Christobel finds Geraldine (detail)
WILLIAM GERSHAM COLLINGWOOD
1854–1932

26

Hot Dates

IF YOU'RE DATING someone for the first time, taking your partner out for a special occasion or simply wanting to re-ignite that flame of passion between you, it helps to understand what would please that person most.

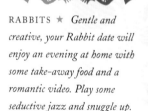

RATS ★ *Wine and dine him or take her to a party. Do something on impulse… go to the races or take a flight in a hot air balloon.*

OXEN ★ *Go for a drive in the country and drop in on a stately home. Visit an art gallery or antique shops. Then have an intimate dinner à deux.*

'So glad to see you…'
COCA-COLA 1945

TIGERS ★ *Tigers thrive on excitement so go clay-pigeon shooting, Formula One racing or challenge each other to a Quasar dual. A date at the theatre will put stars in your Tiger's eyes.*

RABBITS ★ *Gentle and creative, your Rabbit date will enjoy an evening at home with some take-away food and a romantic video. Play some seductive jazz and snuggle up.*

DRAGONS ★ *Mystery and magic will thrill your Dragon date. Take in a son et lumière show or go to a carnival. Or drive to the coast and sink your toes in the sand as the sun sets.*

SNAKES ★ *Don't do anything too active – these creatures like to take life sloooowly. Hire a row-boat for a long, lazy ride down the river. Give a soothing massage, then glide into a sensual jacuzzi together.*

The Carnival
GASTON-DOIN 19/20TH CENTURY

HORSES ★ *Your zany Horse gets easily bored. Take her on a mind-spinning tour of the local attractions. Surprise him with tickets to a musical show. Whatever you do, keep them guessing.*

SHEEP ★ *These folk adore the Arts so visit a museum, gallery or poetry recital. Go to a concert, the ballet, or the opera.*

MONKEYS ★ *The fantastical appeals to this partner, so go to a fancy-dress party or a masked ball, a laser light show or a sci-fi movie.*

ROOSTERS ★ *Grand gestures will impress your Rooster. Escort her to a film première or him to a formal engagement. Dressing up will place this date in seventh heaven.*

DOGS ★ *A cosy dinner will please this most unassuming of partners more than any social occasion. Chatting and story telling will ensure a close understanding.*

PIGS ★ *Arrange a slap-up meal or a lively party, or cruise through the shopping mall. Shopping is one of this partner's favourite hobbies!*

猴

28

*Detail from
Chinese
Marriage
Ceremony*
CHINESE
PAINTING

Year of Commitment

CAN THE YEAR in which you marry (or make a firm commitment to live together) have any influence upon your marital relationship or the life you and your partner forge together? According to the Orientals, it certainly can. Whether your marriage is fiery, gentle, productive, passionate, insular or sociable doesn't so much depend on your animal nature, as on the nature of the Animal in whose year you tied the knot.

IF YOU MARRY IN A YEAR OF THE...

RAT ★ *your marriage should succeed because ventures starting now attract long-term success. Materially, you won't want and life is full of friendship.*

Marriage Feast
CHINESE PAINTING

OX ★ *your relationship will be solid and tastes conventional. Diligence will be recognized and you'll be well respected.*

TIGER ★ *you'll need plenty of humour to ride out the storms. Marrying in the Year of the Tiger is not auspicious.*

RABBIT ★ *you're wedded under the emblem of lovers. It's auspicious for a happy, carefree relationship, as neither partner wants to rock the boat.*

DRAGON ★ *you're blessed. This year is highly auspicious for luck, happiness and success.*

SNAKE ★ *it's good for romance but sexual entanglements are rife. Your relationship may seem languid, but passions run deep.*

HORSE ★ *chances are you decided to marry on the spur of the moment as the Horse year encourages impetuous behaviour. Marriage now may be volatile.*

SHEEP ★ *your family and home are blessed but watch domestic spending. Money is very easily frittered away.*

Marriage Ceremony
CHINESE PAINTING

MONKEY ★ *married life could be unconventional. As plans go awry your lives could be full of surprises.*

ROOSTER ★ *drama characterizes your married life. Your household will run like clockwork, but bickering could strain your relationship.*

DOG ★ *it's a truly fortunate year and you can expect domestic joy. Prepare for a large family as the Dog is the sign of fertility!*

PIG ★ *it's highly auspicious and there'll be plenty of fun. Watch out for indulgence and excess.*

Marriage Ceremony (detail)
CHINESE PAINTING

Detail from Chinese Marriage Ceremony
CHINESE PAINTING

TYPICAL MONKEY PLEASURES

COLOUR PREFERENCES ★ Yellow, gold

Quartz crystal

Agate

Topaz

GEMS AND STONES ★ Quartz crystal, aquamarine, topaz, agate

SUITABLE GIFTS ★ Book tokens, gold pen, mobile phone, personal computer, playing cards, a make-over, joke book, puzzle

HOBBIES AND PASTIMES ★ Playing piano or guitar, table-tennis, poker, word-games, dancing, craft-work, karaoke

HOLIDAY PREFERENCES ★ Not the mountains or plains for you but the city with its bright lights, traffic and hubbub. So it's got to be the Big Apple (New York) or a big, bustling capital. With your luck, why not dice with fate in Monte Carlo or Las Vegas?

Monkeys love Big City energy.

COUNTRIES LINKED WITH THE MONKEY ★ USA, Egypt, Hungary, Portugal, Morocco

The Monkey Parent

HAVING YOU AS A PARENT is more like having another brother or big sister around. They say of you Monkeys that you have Peter Pan qualities, that you retain your youthfulness all your lives and never really grow up. You genuinely enjoy being around children, playing their games, sharing their high spirits, taking part in their discussions. Open-minded and playful, if you're not chatting or telling jokes to your youngsters, you're probably curled up together on the sofa enthralling them with another of your magical stories before bed.

Monkey parents are as enthralled by adventures as their children.

YOUNG AT HEART

Being so young at heart comes in jolly handy as a parent because it means you don't find it difficult to relate to your offspring on their own level. There's no generation gap in your family.

THE MONKEY HABITAT

Without a doubt you're much more suited to the hurly-burly of the city than you are to the peace and quiet of a rural setting. You like to be at the centre of things, where the action is, to feel the pulse of life around you. Seeing people going past your door or watching the crowds throng to the market square will keep you amused for hours. So it's a room with a view that you need from whence to survey the world. A town house, preferably situated on top of a hill and overlooking the centre, would be an ideal Monkey house.

Animal Babies

FOR SOME parents, their children's personalities harmonize perfectly with their own. Others find that no matter how much they may love their offspring they're just not on the same wave-length.

Our children arrive with their characters already well formed and, according to Chinese philosophy, shaped by the influence of their Animal Year. So you should be mindful of the year in which you conceive.

BABIES BORN IN THE YEAR OF THE...

RAT ★ *love being cuddled. They keep on the go – so give them plenty of rest. Later they enjoy collecting things.*

OX ★ *are placid, solid and independent. If not left to their own devices they sulk.*

TIGER ★ *are happy and endearing. As children, they have irrepressible energy. Boys are sporty and girls tom-boys.*

RABBIT ★ *are sensitive and strongly bonded to their mother. They need stability to thrive.*

DRAGON ★ *are independent and imaginative from the start. Encourage any interest that will allow their talents to flourish.*

SNAKE ★ *have great charm. They are slow starters so may need help with school work. Teach them to express feelings.*

猴

One Hundred Children Scroll
ANON, MING PERIOD

HORSE ★ *will burble away contentedly for hours. Talking starts early and they excel in languages.*

SHEEP ★ *are placid, well-behaved and respectful. They are family-oriented and never stray too far from home.*

MONKEY ★ *take an insatiable interest in everything. With agile minds they're quick to learn. They're good-humoured but mischievous!*

ROOSTER ★ *are sociable. Bright and vivacious, their strong adventurous streak best shows itself on a sports field.*

DOG ★ *are cute and cuddly. Easily pleased, they are content just pottering around the house amusing themselves for hours. Common sense is their greatest virtue.*

PIG ★ *are affectionate and friendly. Well-balanced, self-confident children, they're happy-go-lucky and laid-back. They are popular with friends.*

Health, Wealth and Worldly Affairs

AS FAR AS YOU'RE CONCERNED, life's too short to be ill. With your indomitable spirit you tend to keep diseases at bay so you're fighting fit and generally enjoy extraordinarily good health. The medical fraternity scratch their heads in wonder at your amazing powers of recovery. If you do succumb it's likely to be to nervous disorders or, later on, to heart or circulatory conditions, due to the fast pace at which you lead your life.

Grinding routine at the bottom of the heap is not the Monkey way of working.

Just as the Monkey's preferred territory is the uppermost branches of a tree, so at work you like to be at the top. Being in charge comes naturally to the Monkey-born.

CAREER

Adaptability and a good memory are your stock-in-trade. Intelligent and astute, you pick up skills in the twinkling of an eye and then, in two shakes of a duck's tail, you work out a way of improving the task. If a job can be done in half the time for twice the money, you're sure to find the way to do it.

猴

FINANCES

Though you have the knack of making money, and often great heaps of it, you're equally good at spending it. You're not the best saver in the world since you live for the moment and tend to let tomorrow look after itself, so some wise investment now and then wouldn't go amiss.

At work, monotony is the killer. You need a racy, pacy job, with plenty of variety to keep you on your toes. With your brilliant head for business, you're a supreme problem-solver, and a champion wheeler-dealer. Emergencies never faze you since you're one of those people who thrive on pressure.

Monkeys are the life and soul of any party.

FRIENDSHIPS

Sociable and gregarious, your bulging address book testifies to your huge circle of friends and acquaintances. You relish being in company, chatting and sharing the odd joke with your mates and you're a witty and thoroughly entertaining companion.

MONKEYS MAKE EXCELLENT:

★ Scientists ★ Doctors ★ Engineers ★ Writers ★
★ Editors ★ Journalists ★ Air-traffic controllers ★
★ Critics ★ Film directors ★ Actors ★ Croupiers ★
★ Couriers ★ Market traders ★ Jewellers ★
★ Craft workers ★ Financiers ★ Dealers ★
★ Stand-up comedians ★ Sales reps ★ Buyers ★

East Meets West

COMBINE YOUR Oriental Animal sign with your Western Zodiac birth sign to form a deeper and richer understanding of your character and personality.

36

ARIES MONKEY

★ Life is a constant round of social events, meeting new people and talking to your friends. You're a high profile individual, amusing and fun-loving and boredom is your biggest enemy.

TAUREAN MONKEY

★ Part of you wants a steady life and part wants freedom. With an understanding partner to provide a loving environment while allowing you space, you can achieve a happy and settled relationship.

GEMINI MONKEY

★ You're a whizz-kid and magician extraordinaire. You go through life like a whirling dervish, but you're miserable without an adoring partner at your side.

CANCERIAN MONKEY

★ Home-loving, you're responsible and a good provider. Money is important to you and you're a financial wizard. You have a driving libido and are invariably madly in love.

LEONINE MONKEY

★ If there's a spotlight, you'll be smack in the middle of it! You're a terrific attention-seeker because of your need for love and reassurance. In return, you make an adoring partner.

VIRGO MONKEY

★ Security is what you seek and when you find a partner to provide this you respond with devotion. You're formidable in business and successful in life.

猴

37

LIBRAN MONKEY

★ Charm is your superlative asset. With that and your ability to co-operate you're likely to make a successful and loving long-term relationship. Only as part of a partnership do you feel truly balanced and whole.

SCORPIO MONKEY

★ Devious and intense, you're a lusty lover with a mega urge for sex. Deeply passionate and devoted to the object of your affections, you're possessive and jealous and make it your mission to get even with anyone who dares cross you in love.

SAGITTARIAN MONKEY

★ An easy blend producing a lucky, cheerful personality albeit clever and deep-thinking. You won't want to settle down too early in life because there's such a lot to see and do first. It's debatable whether you're ever really prepared to put relationships above your worldly ambitions.

CAPRICORN SHEEP

★ Intelligent and hardworking, you're more stable and resolute than most Monkeys. Image and status are driving forces in your life, so you'll be selective in your search for the perfect partner. Once found, you look no further.

AQUARIAN MONKEY

★ Colourful and eccentric is perhaps the best way to describe you. Bright and breezy, it's a sharing of minds you're after in a relationship, not a sharing of hearts; for you, sex is just another form of communication between two people.

PISCEAN MONKEY

★ There's a whimsical delicacy about you that belies a clever, calculating mind. Women are femmes fatales and men have a certain mystique that attracts potential suitors to them like bees to honey. Ideally, you want an easy, pampered life, so you'll choose a partner who can provide one.

猴

FAMOUS MONKEYS

Princess Caroline of Monaco

Diana Ross

Rod Stewart

Elizabeth Taylor

Kiri Te Kanawa

Bette Davis

Elizabeth Taylor ★ Rod Stewart ★ Jacqueline Bisset
Jason Donovan ★ Michael Douglas ★ Tom Hanks
Princess Caroline of Monaco ★ Mick Jagger
Johnny Cash ★ Jerry Hall ★ Diana Ross
Kiri Te Kanawa ★ Fellini ★ Bette Davis
Leonardo da Vinci ★ Charles Dickens
Harry Truman ★ Gauguin
Nelson Rockefeller ★ Jacques Tati
Modigliani ★ James Stewart

Charles Dickens

The Monkey Year in Focus

IN THE YEAR OF THE MONKEY, nothing is straightforward. Try as we might to attend to every detail, somewhere along the line something will happen to make our plans come unstuck. What we can expect, however, is the unexpected.

GREMLINS

Gremlins abound. Buying or selling, going on holiday or organizing a bash, check your insurance policies carefully and have alternative plans tucked up your sleeves. A decided undercurrent of instability pervades the economy, undermining governments and international politics. Fast talking and sharp wits win the day.

A SWINGING YEAR

The year has an upbeat, progressive swing. The world of communications will have its heyday and all the industries that depend on mental or manual dexterity will make progress under the influence of the Monkey's agile intelligence.

ACTIVITIES ASSOCIATED WITH THE MONKEY YEAR

The discovery, invention, patenting, marketing, manufacturing or first occasion of: liquid helium, Bakelite, the sub-machine gun, radio astronomy, the Zippo lighter, mobiles, neutrinos and astronauts orbiting the Moon.

Your Monkey Fortunes
for the Next 12 Years

1996 MARKS THE BEGINNING of a new 12-year cycle in the Chinese calendar. How your relationships and worldly prospects fare will depend on the influence of each Animal year in turn.

1996 YEAR OF THE RAT	*19 Feb 1996 – 6 Feb 1997*

Use the good auspices of the Rat year to expand your ideas, to further ambitions and to promote projects that are close to your heart. It's a lucky time and gives you every opportunity to succeed in almost anything you attempt.

YEAR TREND: GO FOR IT!

1997 YEAR OF THE OX	*7 Feb 1997 – 27 Jan 1998*

Consolidation is the name of the game this year; work will slow down giving you time to concentrate on your personal life. Put future plans on hold while you spend quality time with those you love.

YEAR TREND: MODERATE PROGRESS

1998 YEAR OF THE TIGER	*28 Jan 1998 – 15 Feb 1999*

Tiger years are never easy times for you and pushing yourself or your plans forward now will only attract hostility. Under such unfavourable conditions, your best bet is just to work as steadily and calmly as you can.

YEAR TREND: KEEP A LOW PROFILE

1999 YEAR OF THE RABBIT · *16 Feb 1999 – 4 Feb 2000*

A brighter year than last; the forces are with you. New ideas will be favourably received and opportunities arise unexpectedly. There are excellent auguries for moving, or refurbishing your home.

YEAR TREND: CREATIVITY BRINGS SUCCESS

41

2000 YEAR OF THE DRAGON · *5 Feb 2000 – 23 Jan 2001*

Everything about the Dragon year is conducive to your mentality and ambitions. You're able to put your ideas across confidently and your efforts will bring success: recognition and career advancement are assured. A romantic meeting promises enduring love.

YEAR TREND: THRILLING

In the Year of the Dragon, the Monkey can aim high.

2001 YEAR OF THE SNAKE · *24 Jan 2001 – 11 Feb 2002*

Although you'll make headway, behind-the-scenes activity may well undermine progress in your career. Be aware or else you could find yourself pipped at the post at the very last minute. Relationships are equally unsettled but friends see you through.

YEAR TREND: DISAPPOINTING

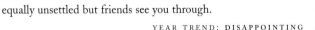

猴

2002 YEAR OF THE HORSE *12 Feb 2002 – 31 Jan 2003*

A fortunate year with some lucky opportunities, and perhaps a windfall could land in your lap. You'll enjoy the fast tempo of events but are warned to moderate over-confidence and impulsive action.

YEAR TREND: GENERALLY FORTUITOUS

2003 YEAR OF THE SHEEP *1 Feb 2003 – 21 Jan 2004*

Occupationally, this year will bring plenty of opportunity for making money, for travelling and for widening your network of contacts. The down side is that relationships could prove to be bugbears unless you think before you speak.

YEAR TREND: LET SLEEPING DOGS LIE

2004 YEAR OF THE MONKEY *22 Jan 2004 – 8 Feb 2005*

In this, your own year, you'll be Mr or Ms Popular with friends and acquaintances seeking out your company. If you're looking for that special person with whom to spend the rest of your life, you could well find him or her now.

YEAR TREND: A TIME OF REAL PROGRESS

猴

In the Year of the Rooster, the Monkey can make business a pleasure.

2005 YEAR OF THE ROOSTER *9 Feb 2005 – 28 Jan 2006*

If you put in the work you can be sure that your efforts will be repaid handsomely this year. Mix pleasure with business to relieve the hectic schedule that 2005 has in store. Love, relationships and emotions are stable.

YEAR TREND: BUSY AND CONSTRUCTIVE

2006 YEAR OF THE DOG *29 Jan 2006 – 17 Feb 2007*

The pace continues relentlessly and though luck is on your side, you are advised to scrutinize the small print in any business dealings as fraud and trickery are about this year. It's an auspicious time for marriage.

YEAR TREND: IF IN DOUBT, LEAVE IT OUT

2007 YEAR OF THE PIG *18 Feb 2007 – 6 Feb 2008*

Carelessness and impatience dog your steps this year but as long as you don't rest on your laurels, all should go well for you. Application and an astute sense of timing, however, will ensure success. Relationships warm the heart.

YEAR TREND: CARE AND ATTENTION BRING RESULTS

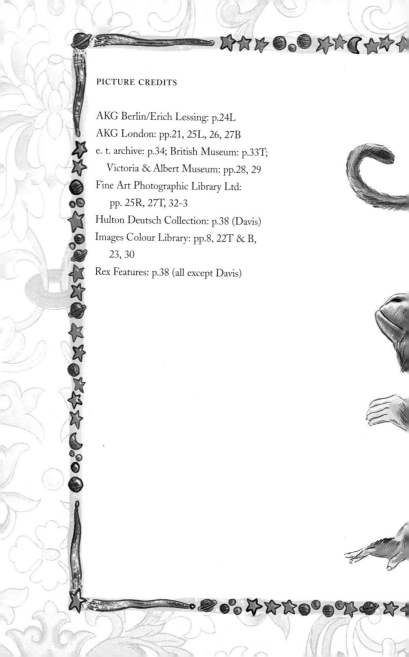